A-Z CHELTENHAM &

C000221130

CONTENT

REFERENCE

Motorway	**M5**		Car Park (Selected)	P
Road	A38		Church or Chapel	†
Road	B4008		Cycleway (Selected)	🚲
ual Carriageway			Fire Station	■
One-way Street			Hospital	H
traffic flow on A Roads is also indicated by a heavy line on the driver's left.			House Numbers (Selected roads)	13 8 3
nder Construction Road			Information Centre	i
opening dates correct at time of publication.			National Grid Reference	387
roposed Road			Park & Ride	Javelin P+
estricted Access			Police Station	▲
edestrianized Road			Post Office	★
rack / Footpath			Safety Camera with Speed Limit	(30)
esidential Walkway			Fixed cameras and long term road work cameras Symbols do not indicate camera direction	
ailway	Level Crossing / Station / Tunnel / Heritage Station		Toilet without facilities for the Disabled	▽
			with facilities for the Disabled	▽
uilt-up Area	BATH ST		Viewpoint	🔆 ☀
ocal Authority Boundary	— · — · —		Educational Establishment	▨
osttown Boundary	——————		Hospital or Healthcare Building	▨
ostcode Boundary (within Posttown)	— — — —		Industrial Building	▨
			Leisure or Recreational Facility	▨
Map Continuation	28 Large Scale Page 4		Place of Interest	▨
			Public Building	▨
			Shopping Centre or Market	▨
			Other Selected Buildings	▨

SCALE

Map Pages 6-56	Map Pages 4 & 5
1:15,840 4 inches (10.16 cm) to 1 mile, 6.31 cm to 1 km	1:7,920 8 inches (20.32 cm) to 1 mile, 12.63 cm to 1 km
0 ¼ ½ Mile	0 ⅛ ¼ Mile
0 250 500 750 Metres	0 100 200 300 400 Metres

Copyright of Geographers' A-Z Map Company Limited

Fairfield Road, Borough Green, Sevenoaks, Kent TN15 8PP
Telephone: 01732 781000 (Enquiries & Trade Sales)
01732 783422 (Retail Sales)

www.az.co.uk

Copyright © Geographers' A-Z Map Co. Ltd.

Edition 5   2012

OS Ordnance Survey® This product includes mapping data licensed from Ordnance Survey® with the permission of the Controller of Her Majesty's Stationery Office.

© Crown Copyright 2011. All rights reserved. Licence number 100017302

Safety camera information supplied by www.PocketGPSWorld.com

Speed Camera Location Database Copyright 2011 © PocketGPSWorld.com

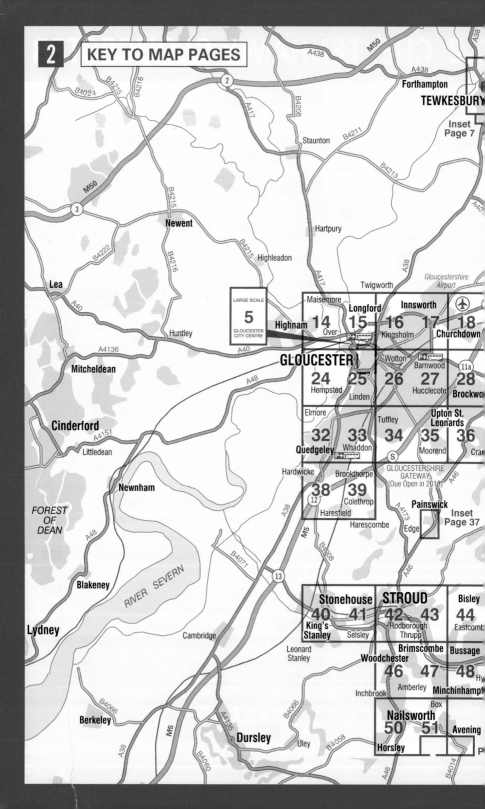

2 KEY TO MAP PAGES

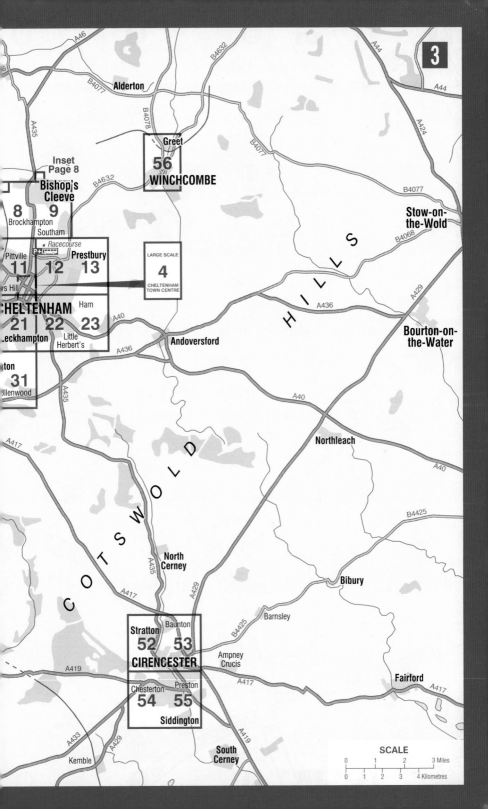

3

Alderton

Greet

56
WINCHCOMBE

Stow-on-
the-Wold

Inset
Page 8

Bishop's
Cleeve

8   **9**

Brockhampton

Southam

Racecourse

P+

Pittville

LARGE SCALE

4

CHELTENHAM
TOWN CENTRE

11   **12**   **Prestbury**

13

Bourton-on-
the-Water

ws Hill

CHELTENHAM   Ham

21   **22**   **23**

eckhampton

Little
Herbert's

Andoversford

ton

31

llenwood

Northleach

North
Cerney

Bibury

Barnsley

Stratton   Baunton

52   **53**

CIRENCESTER

Ampney
Crucis

Fairford

Chesterton   Preston

54   **55**

Siddington

Kemble

South
Cerney

COTSWOLD

HILLS

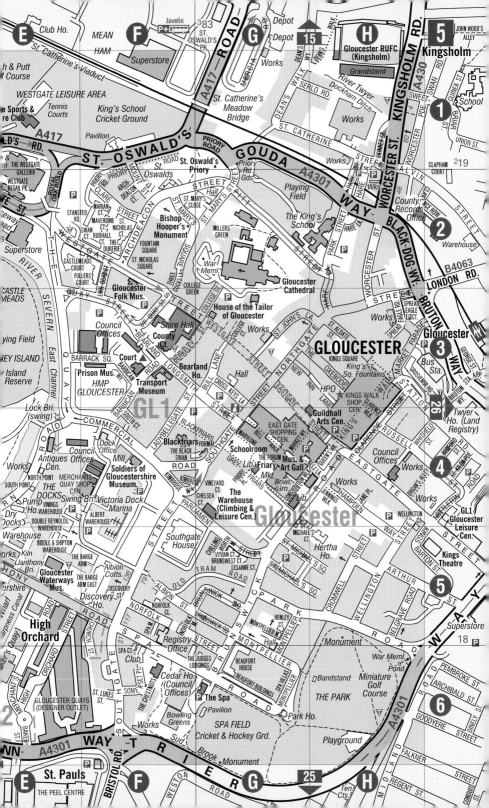

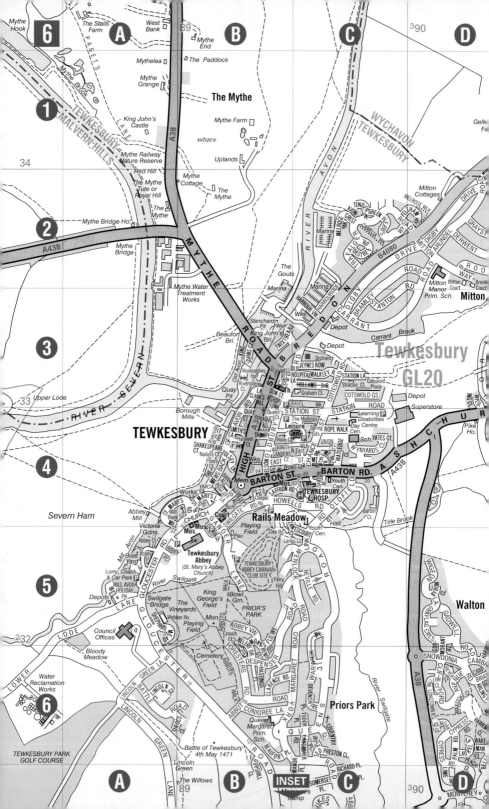

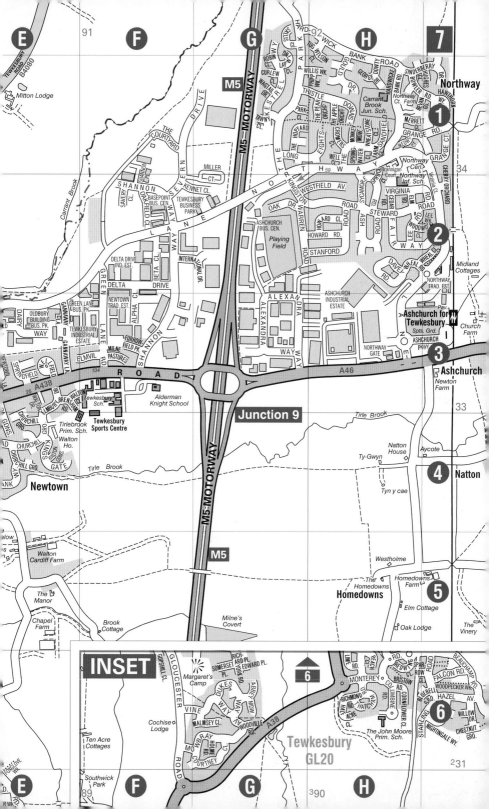

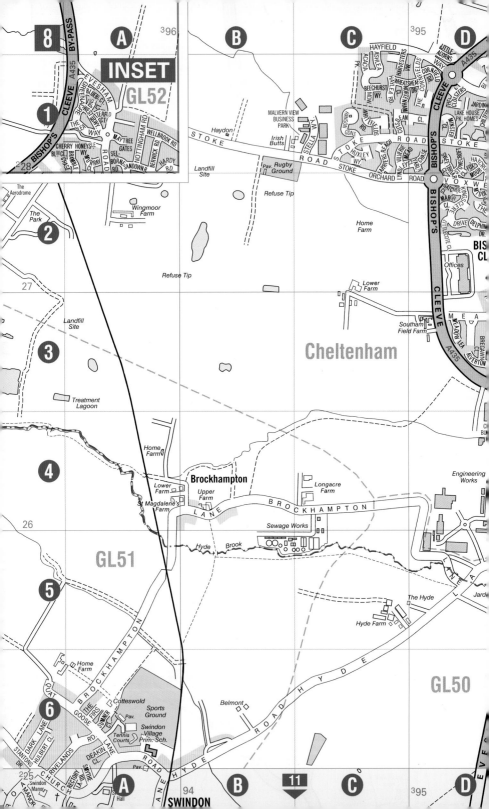

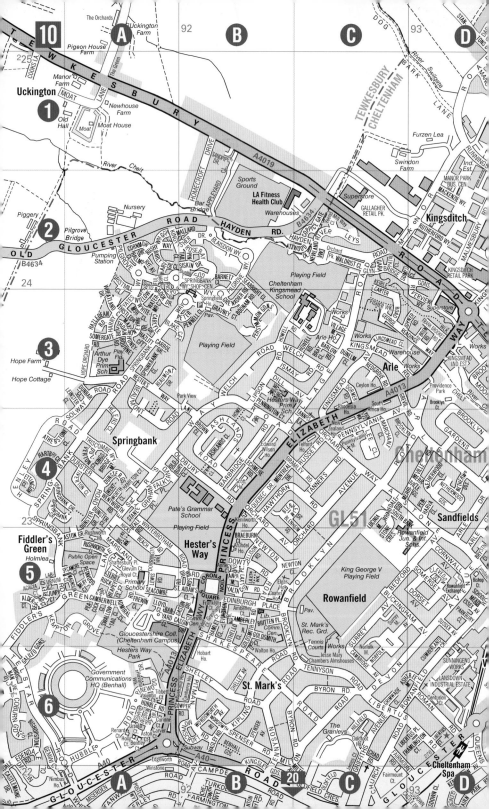

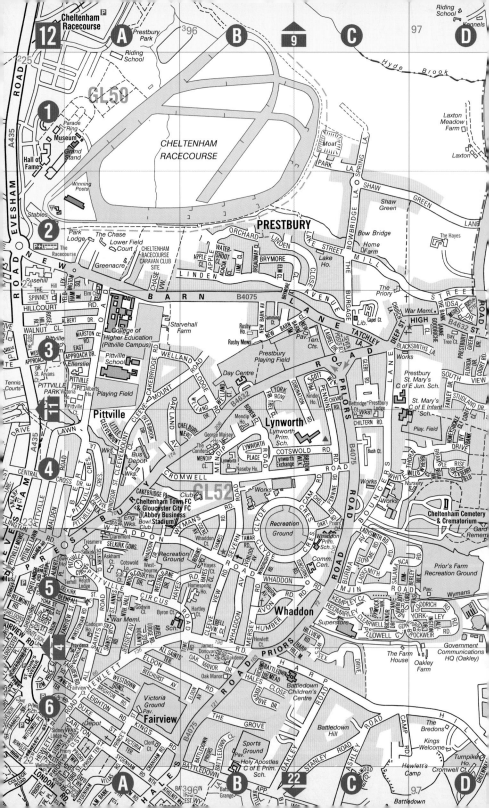

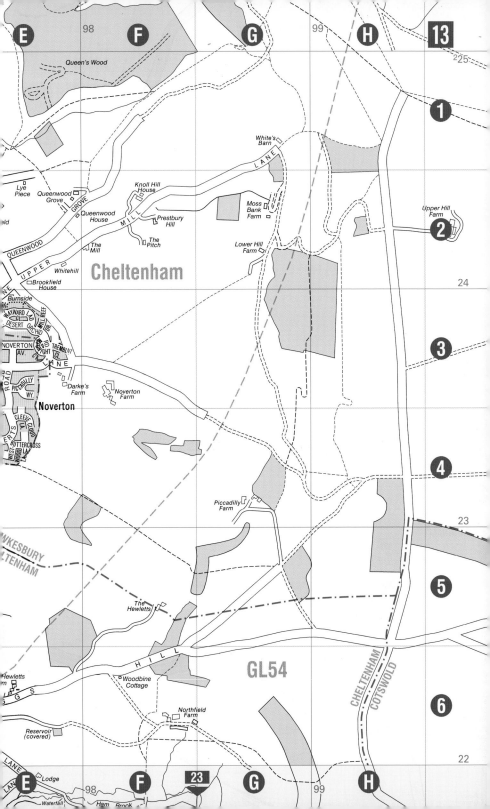

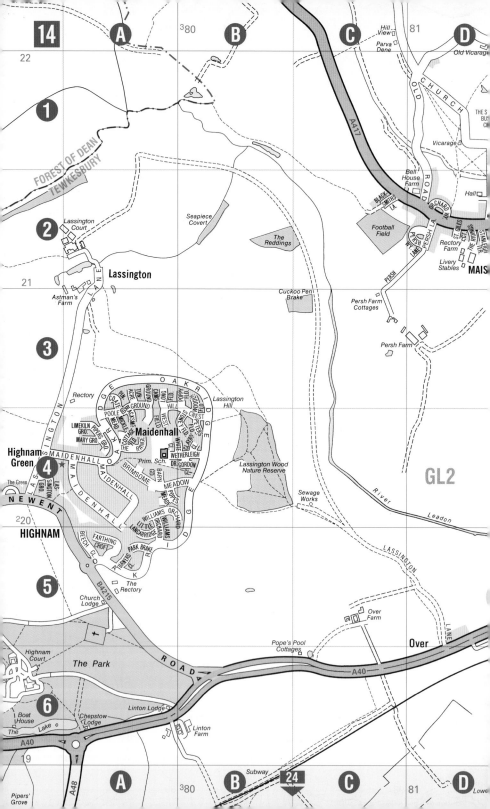

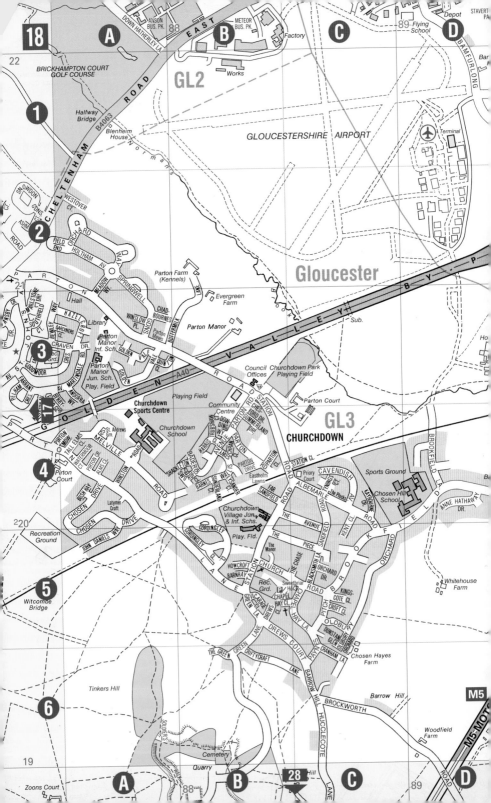

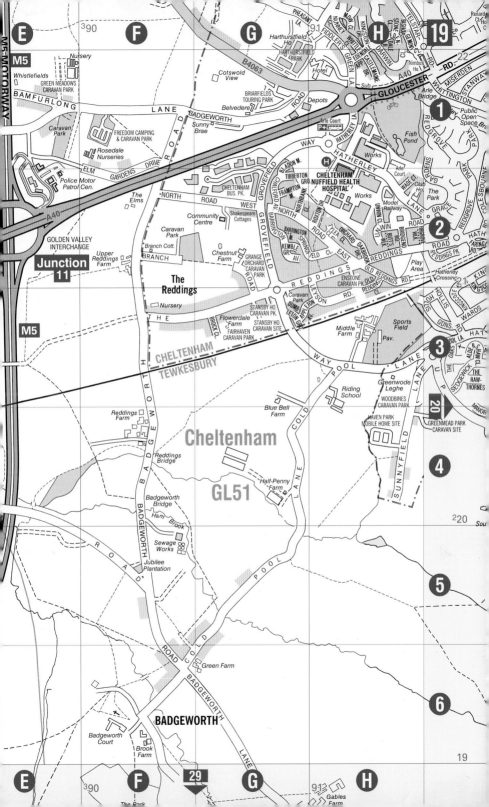

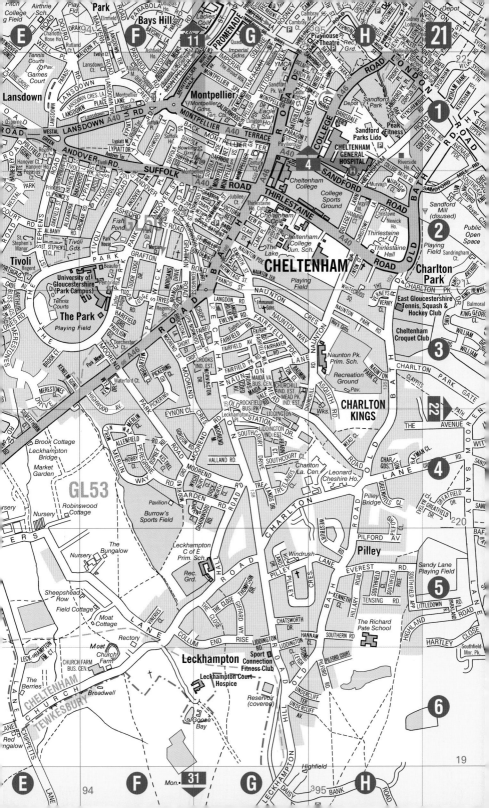

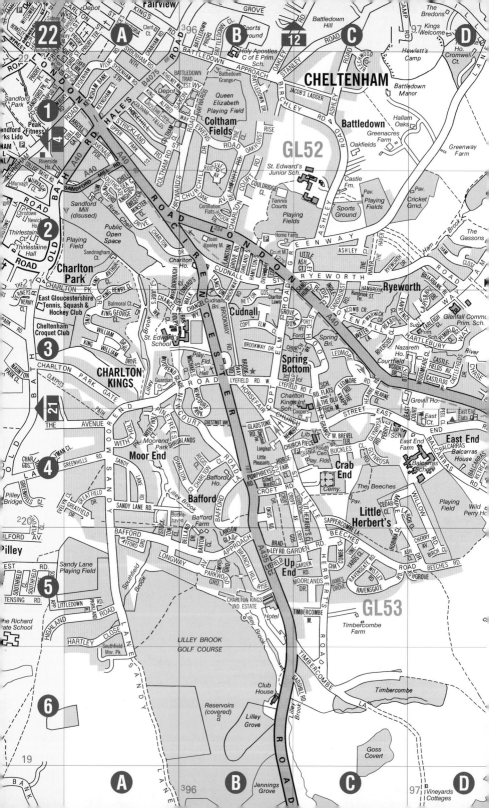

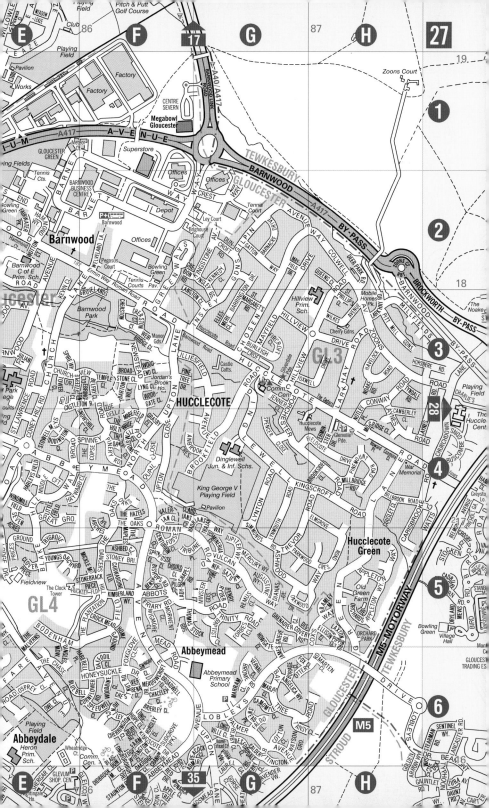

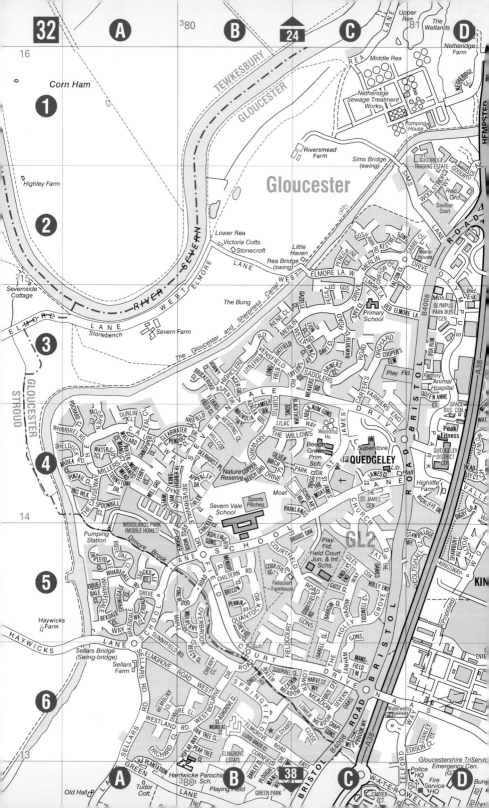

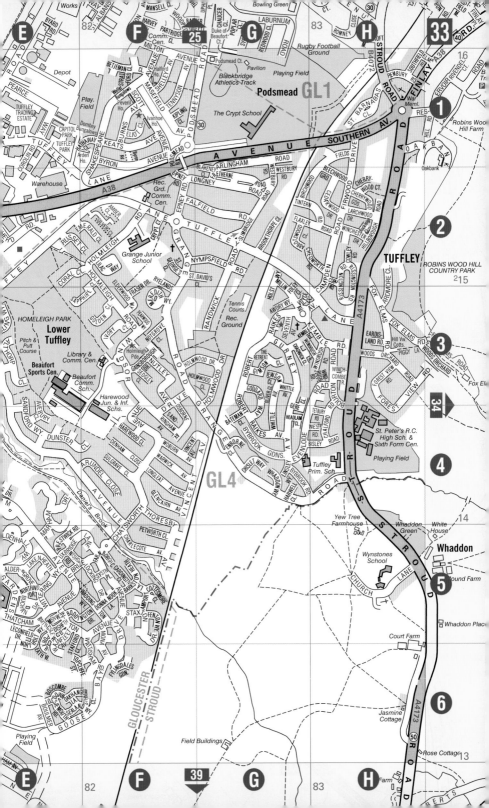

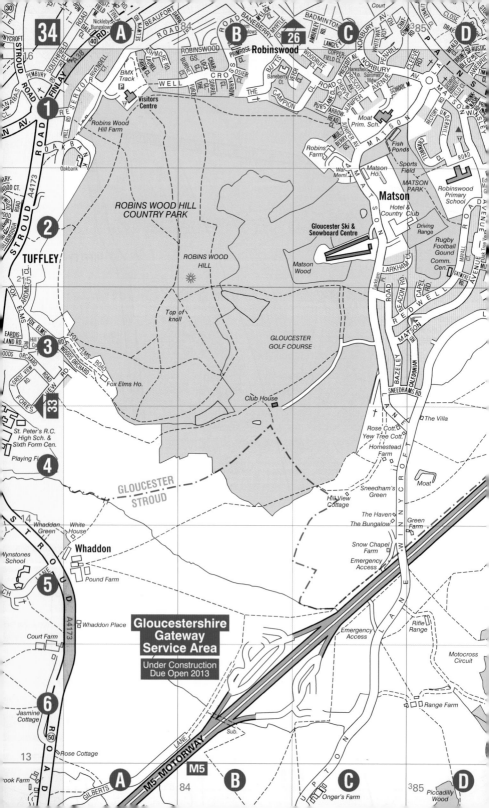

34

A **B** **26** Robinswood **C** **D**

1

Visitors Centre
Robins Wood Hill Farm
BMX Track P
Oakbank

ROBINS WOOD HILL COUNTRY PARK

Robins Farm
War. Meml.
Moat Prim. Sch.
Matson Ho.
Sports Field
MATSON PARK
Fish Ponds
Robinswood Primary School

Matson

2

TUFFLEY

ROBINS WOOD HILL

Gloucester Ski & Snowboard Centre
Matson Wood

Hotel & Country Club
Driving Range
Rugby Football Ground
Comm. Cen.

3

Top of knoll
Fox Elms Ho.

GLOUCESTER GOLF COURSE

33

St. Peter's R.C. High Sch. & Sixth Form Cen.
Playing Fi

Club House

The Villa
Rose Cott.
Yew Tree Cott.
Homestead Farm

4

GLOUCESTER STROUD

Whaddon Green
White House

Whaddon

Wynstones School

Hill View Cottage
Sneedham's Green
The Haven
The Bungalow
Snow Chapel Farm
Emergency Access

Moat
Green Farm

5

Pound Farm

Whaddon Place

Gloucestershire Gateway Service Area
Under Construction
Due Open 2013

Emergency Access

Rifle Range

Motocross Circuit

6

Court Farm

Jasmine Cottage

Rose Cottage

Range Farm

Piccadilly Wood

A **M5** M5-MOTORWAY **B** **C** Onger's Farm **D**

Brook Farm
GILBERTS
Sub.
UPTON

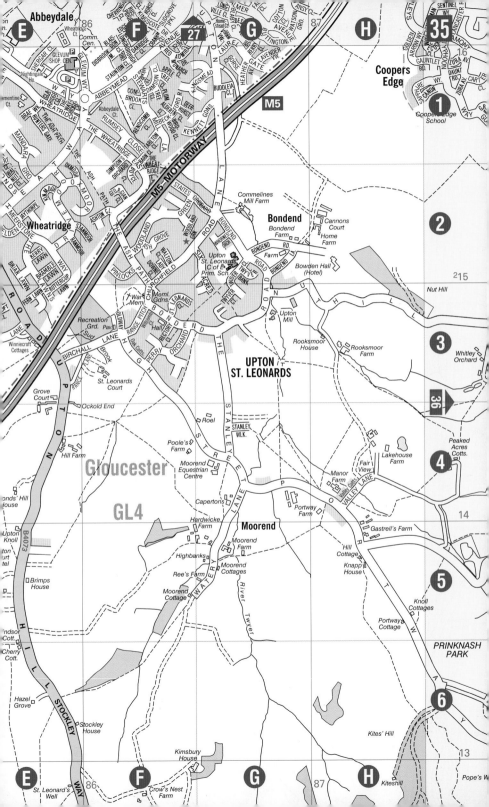

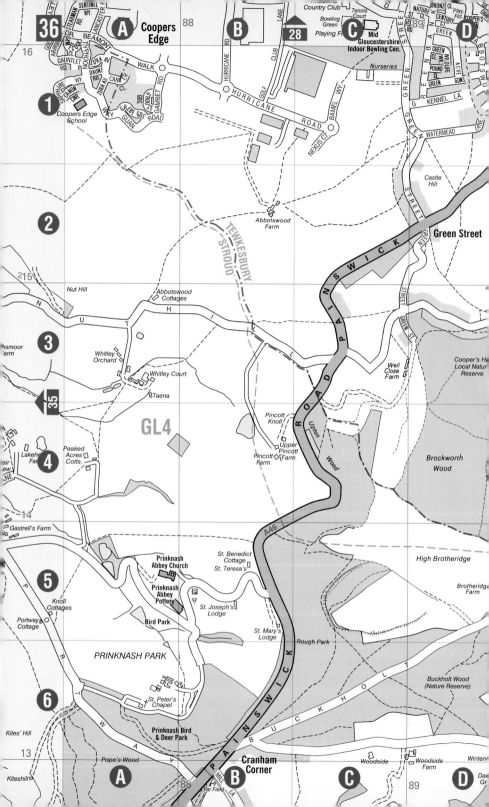

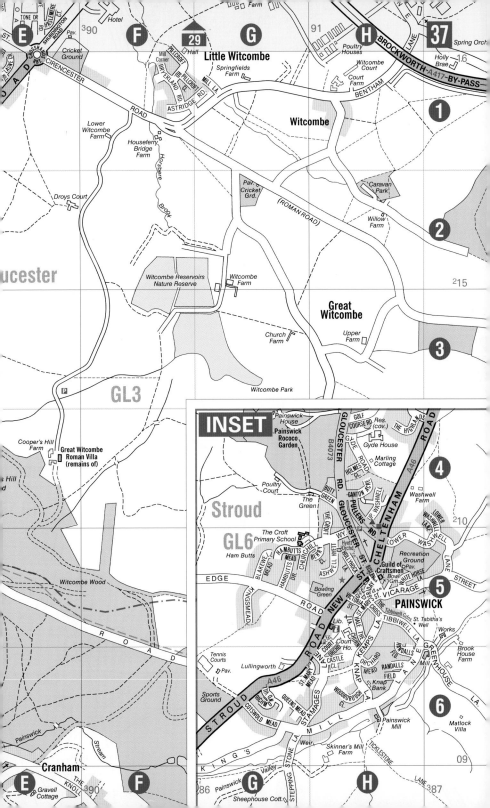

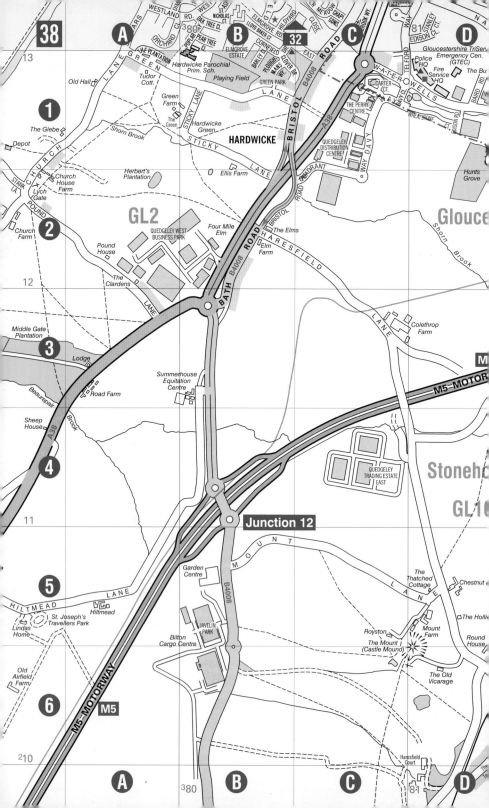

E   82   **F**   Field Buildings   **33**   **G**   83   **H**   **39**

Cottage

GOOSE

Playing Field

Naas Lane

Works

Brunel Ct

Henson Dr

Naas Crossing (foot)

Naas Farm

Naas Lane

GLOUCESTER STROUD

Gypsy Park

Pentrif

GL4

M5

M5 MOTORWAY

Brook Farm

Gilberts Lane

Stroud Road

A4173

1

Brookthorpe Court

2

BROOKTHORPE

St Andrew's Cl

Wyn-Stones Dr

Hill Mead Lane

13

12

Birch Cottages

Withyrows

3

Haresfield Lane

Styles Lane

Styles Farm

Chamber's Farm

Funnels Cottage

Orchard View

Longacre

Daniel's Brook Cottages

4

Daniel's Brook

11

The Lessoms

The Bakehouse

Colethrop Villas

Colethrop Cottage

Cross Farm

Colethrop

5

Colethorpe Court Farm

Hollock House

Threshold Farm

Dewcroft

Stocks Farm

6

Teekles Court

Hayes Farm

HARESCOMBE

Gravel Court Farm

Brook Farm

210

...SFIELD

E   College Farm   82   **F**   **G**   83   **H**

...es Cott

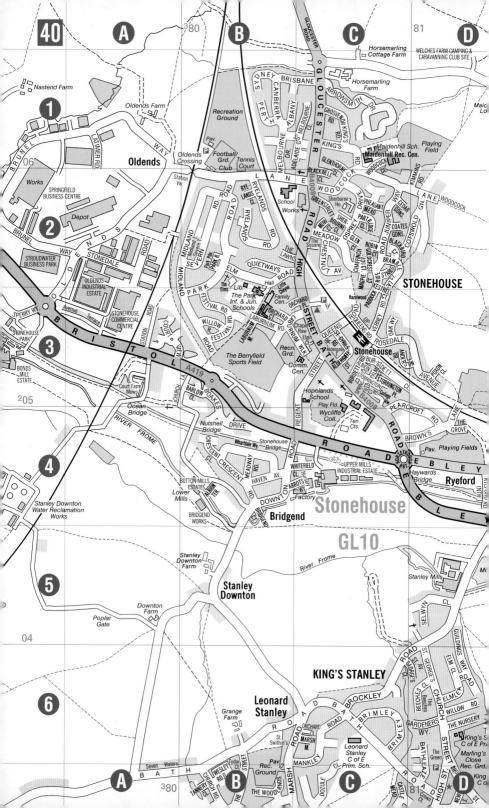

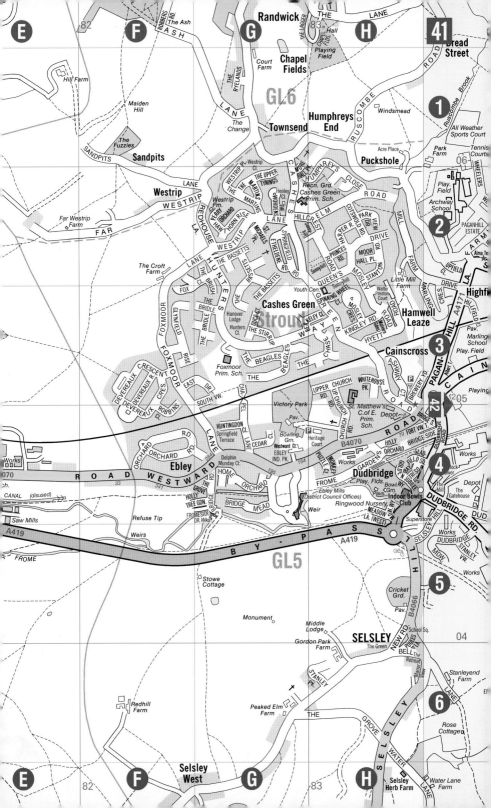

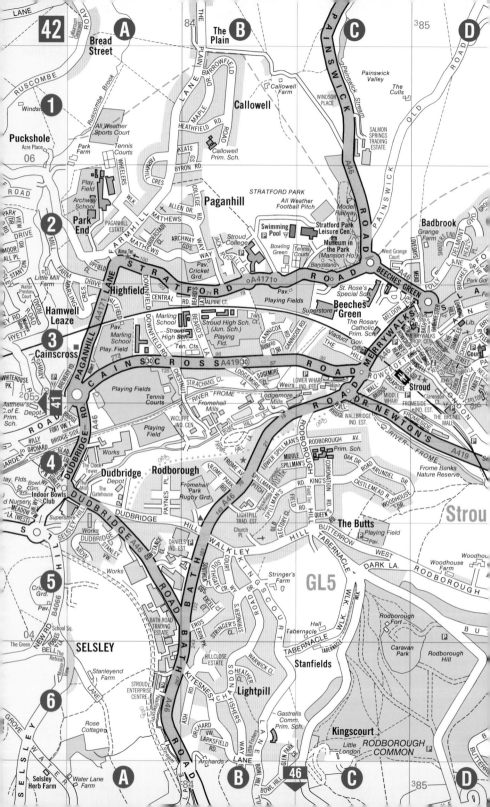

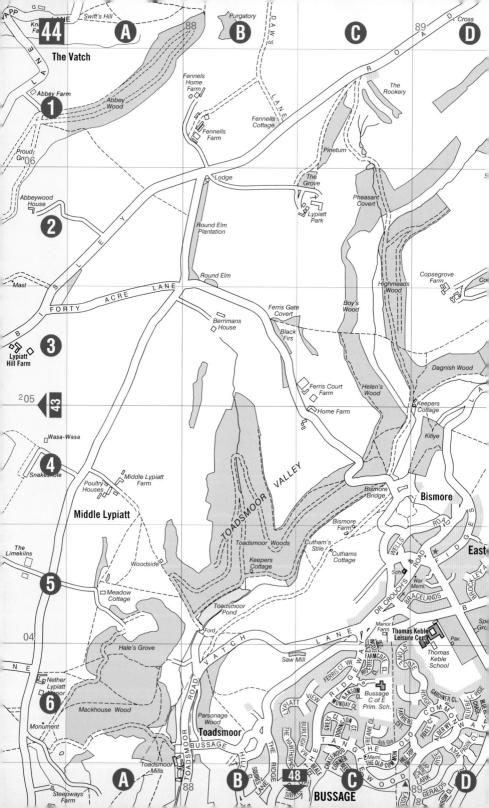

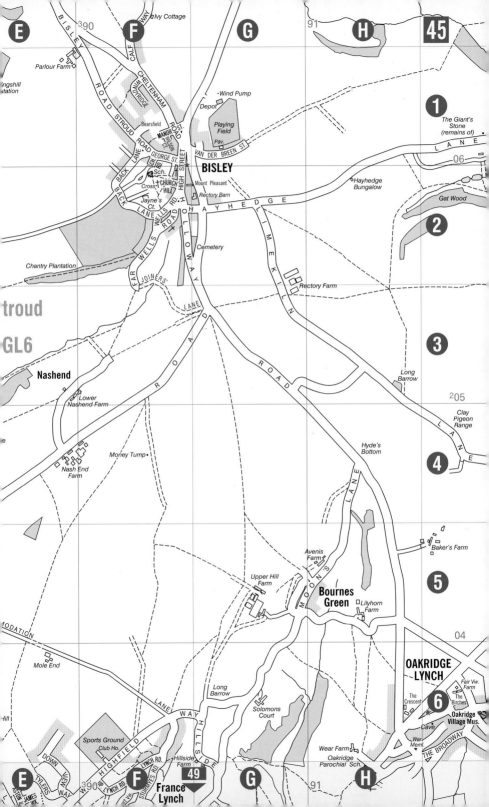

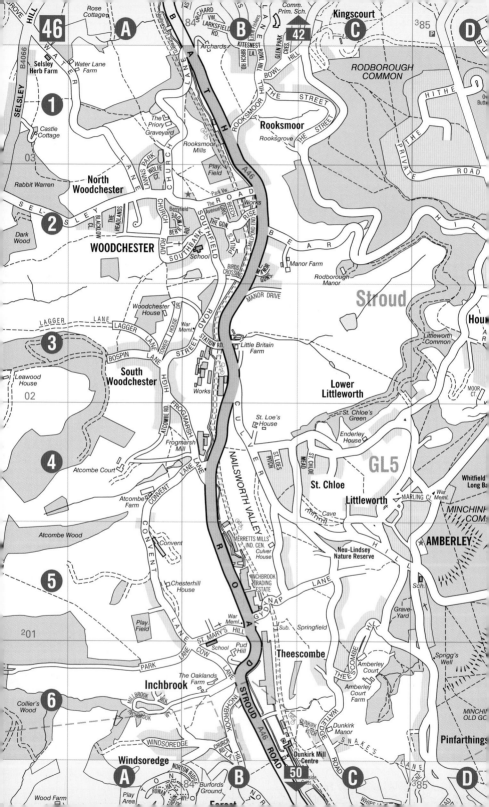

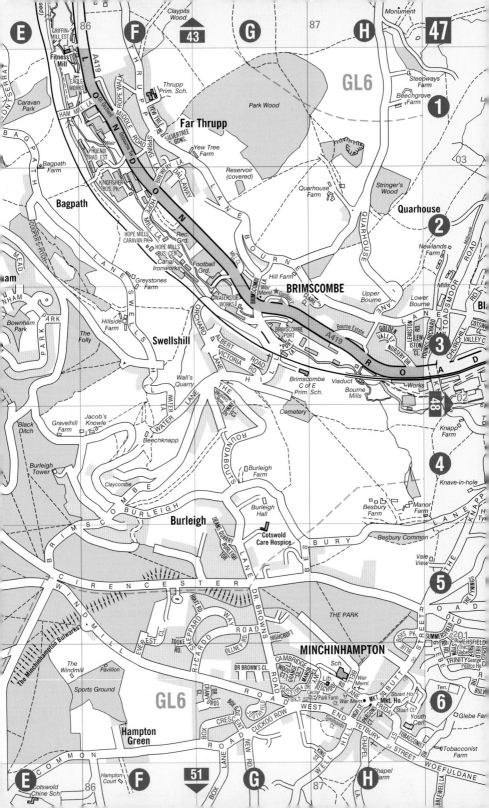

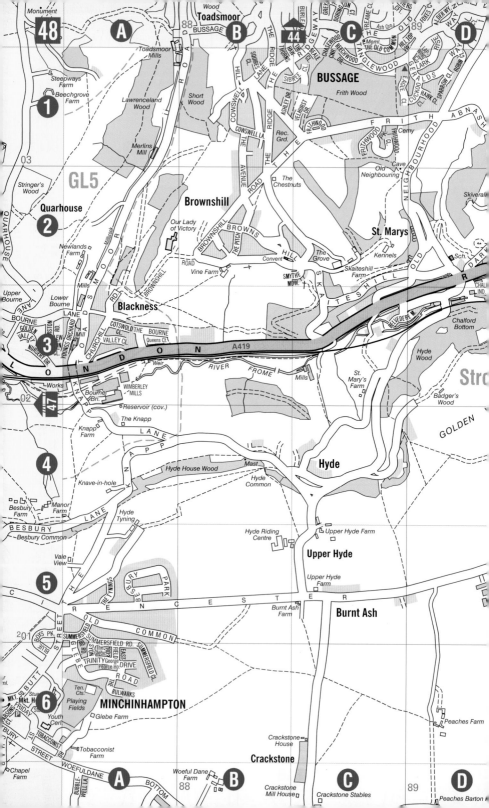

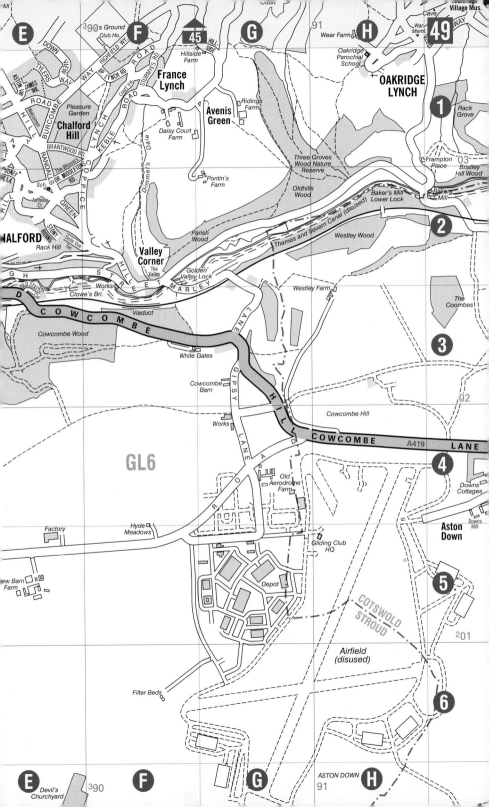

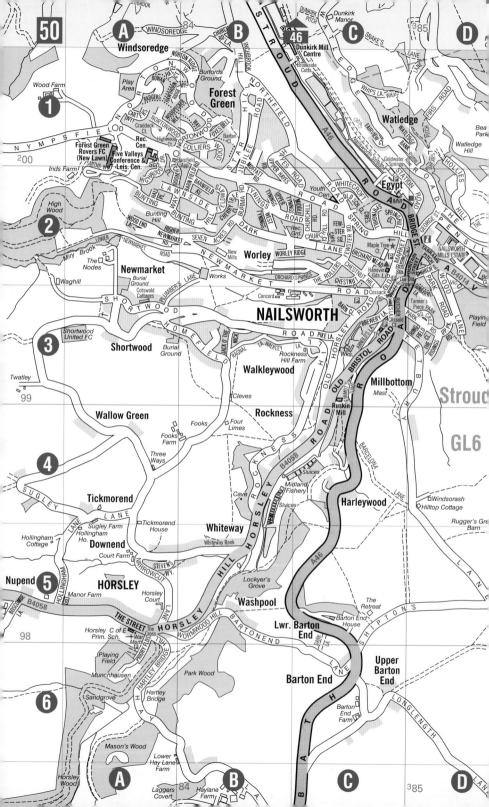

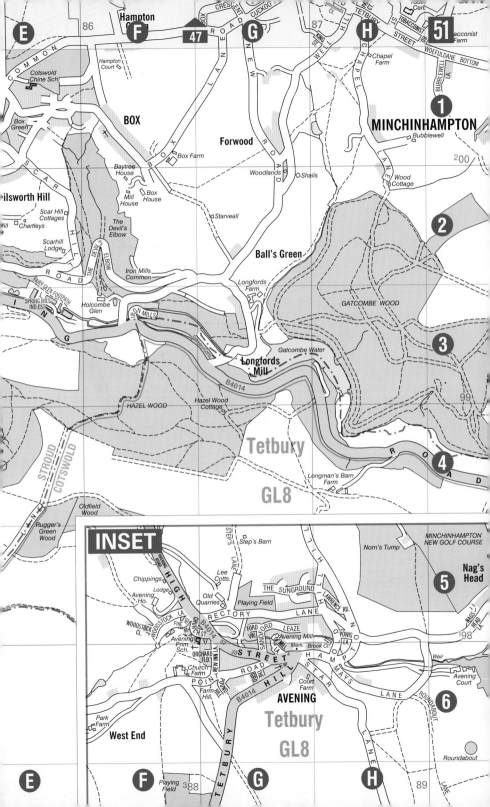

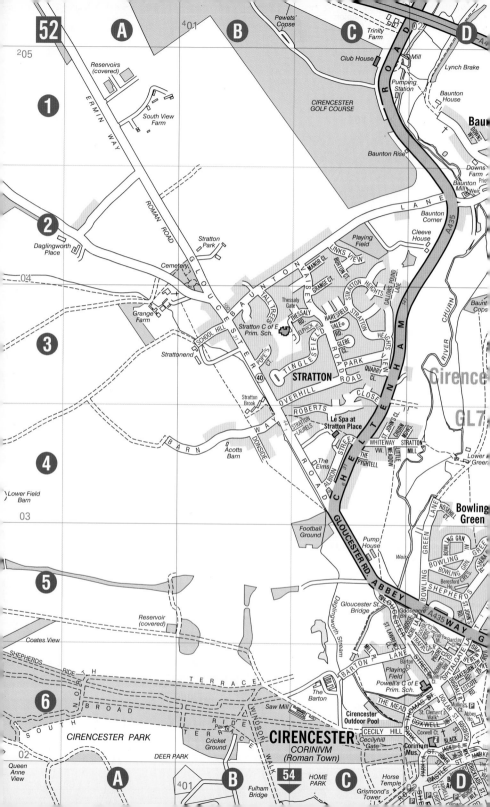

E   03   F   Eldon Wood   G   04   Plantation Strip   H   **53**   205

Exhibition Barn

Wiggold Farm

Wiggold

Raggedhedge Covert

Lower Wiggold House

1

Field Barn Cottage

Wiggold Cottages

New Plantation

Shooters Hill

ROMAN ROAD

FOSSE WAY

2

Coronation Cover   04

Fosse Cottage

Whiteway Farm

Dentice Bushes

Rats Castle

A429

Abbey Home Farm

3

WHITE WAY

Preston Field Barn

Yellow School Copse

A417

Whitelands Wood

ROAD

Galley Hill

4

HARE BUSHES

Whiteway Court

Stow Lodge

ROMAN ROAD   B4425   STREET   03

Kennels

AKEMAN

Hunters Care Centre

CHERRYTREE

ROMAN ROAD

5

Lower Norcote Cottage

Cricket Ground

Pav.

FOSSE WAY

A429

ORMOND

Depot

Elm Tree Cottage

Norcote

Norcote Barn

Norcote House

BURFORD ROAD

ROMAN ROAD

MOSS WY.   IVORY WY.

WINSTONE GS.   WHITESHILL

Norcote Workshops

A419 LANE

LONDON ROAD   A417

6

Corinium Town Wall

CORINIUM

GATE   PAISLEY

ARNOLDS WY.   FOSSE

CHURCHILL

QUEEN   ST.   31   19   58

CENTURY

MILL   MELVILLE

PARTRIDGE WY.   PHEASANT

Norcote Cottages

Beech Grove Court   WHITELANDS RD.   BLUE QUARRY RD.

THE GREEN   SAXON RD.   ABBOTS RD.   PARTRIDGE WY.   WAY

Cirencester Kingshill School

Norcote Cottages

UPPER CHURNSIDE   CHURCHILL   AKEMAN   ST.   KINGSHILL LANE

The Beeches

ROAD

02

E   03   F   **55**   G   04   H

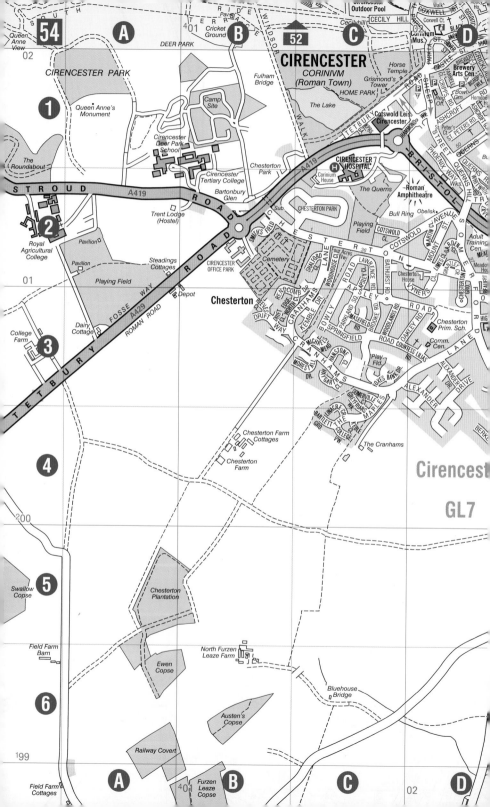

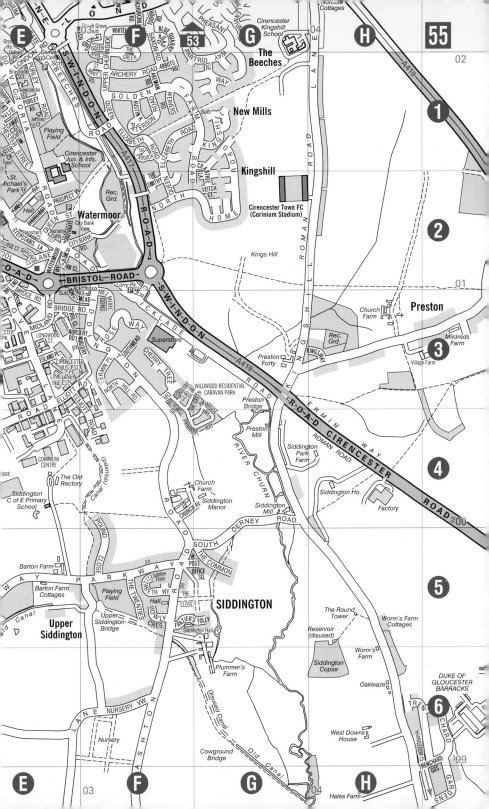